31 DAYS Life changing Journal

By M K Brown

This book is dedicated to my beautiful daughter Lizzie, my parents Lesley and Barry Newton, and my wonderful husband, Steven Brown.

My amazing Aunty Jo who knew I needed to speak to someone and gave me the details of someone for when I was ready.

Also, a recognition to Lorraine and Tig who helped me through the difficult times at the beginning of my new journey.

Contents:

Foreword

"I have known Maxine almost all my life becoming her aunt at the age of seven and I can still recall the envy of the other girls in the playground with some pleasure. I've watched her grow and live through some good times, fairly average times and the sort of time I didn't know how anyone could get through in one piece- this book holds some of the answers to that.

One quality resonates in all my memories of Maxine and that's a single-minded determination to accomplish what she sets her mind to, be that creating a new life on a bat or a path for others to follow to guide them back from grief or dark times.

The first time I saw this quality was when Maxine aged about five cleared a swathe of the pool as she learned to swim shouting "excuse me I'm trying" to anyone foolish enough to be in her way.

It's been a good mantra to see her through this last decade as she has rebuilt her life and healed a heart broken by grief and betrayal. This recovery she's not just done for herself but done in a way that's meant she can offer the steps and tools she has used so others can use them in a book which like her is the perfect mix of compassion and practicality and I'm even prouder to be asked to introduce it to you with the wish it helps you on your journey as I felt in the playground half a century ago.

Love

Jo

Grief is like a private club no one wants to be in.

My Story – Coming out the other side.

My story started in October 2009 Lizzie my daughter had been out partying and stayed at her friends for the weekend. I was packing to go to London as I'd started a new job and I was having to go there for training. I had just packed my car and I was literally going to be leaving in the next half an hour when my mobile went and it was Lizzie's number, I answered with my usual Hey what's up to find it was her best friend Jussy on the other end of the phone. She explained that Lizzie wasn't well, and they had called an ambulance. She told me Lizzie was being put into the back of an ambulance as she just was not responsive, and very poorly I dropped everything, and with my husband I drove frantically to Worksop hospital. We beat the ambulance there; it was a waiting game for as each ambulance that came in seeing if it was Lizzie. Eventually she arrived we went into the accident and emergency where they put us into the relative's room. They would not let us go and see her, but we found out that they were working on her. This must have been about an hour or even been more as time became a blur eventually, we were allowed to see her. She was not responsive, and it was heart breaking to be put back into the waiting room, it was a waiting game the doctor came to see us and explained that she was very poorly they were not sure what was the matter, but at this time the best thing to do was to put her into an induced coma on a life support machine. It was both scary and heart breaking, but we had to put our trust in them and support their treatment of Lizzie who although she was nearly twenty still felt like my baby girl. We had to do that to make sure they could work on her and find out what was the matter.

After many hours they said that it was her diabetes but also there was something else as well, but they were still not sure what. They took blood test after blood test along with other procedures and they suggested we went home to get some rest.

Being told to leave your child in the hospital was a really difficult thing home we went and even ate something before I felt drawn back this time alone as my husband said he could not cope and would come in later.

I spoke to the doctor, and they were still unsure what was going on as they waited for more results. I rang my parents and next thing I knew my mummy by Lizzie's bed with me.

Lizzie was a fiercely bright young woman she worked hard for three mobile, as well as going to college doing a managerial degree business course.

I stepped into a rhythm of popping home, trying to sleep or eat and getting back as soon as I could. Her father popped in as and when. Wednesday, we found out that she had got swine flu, it had been in the UK for a few months and looking back I believe this is what everyone even the doctors had called a bad cold.

Just the week before Lizzie had her injections against flu and swine flu. I had nagged her to double check its ok to have both injections as she wasn't well. She phoned me later to say she'd had them both done and that it was ok even with a cold. We even had a giggle when she said how painful her arms were, but we did not think anything else of it.

So, the good thing was the doctors knew what they are treating now. Now Lizzie started to be barrier nursed so it was full masks and gowns when we went in to see her because it was another wall that stopped me getting close to her. On Thursday or Friday of that week when she had been in an induced coma for about four days, they decided to start slowly waking her up to see how she was. Such a scary time! Mummy and I stood at the side of Lizzie talking to her because that's what the doctor recommended in case she could hear even if she couldn't respond. She had been twitching and the odd eye opening. When suddenly, she just opened both her eyes and tried to sit up, for some reason mummy and I ran in terror calling for help like something from an episode of ghost busters, we didn't even dare to go back into start with until a nurse coaxed us in and explained it was a normal part of waking up. both mummy and I ran out of the room asking for help it was so scary we did not go back in straight away. The nurse came out and said its ok, it is part of waking up.

A little later Lizzie seemed to panic then ask, "Am I blind" When I realised, she couldn't see I could no longer hold back the tears. Luckily, my mother pointed out it might be that she just wasn't wearing her glasses. Lizzie had been short sighted since verry little. She put them on and announced all was well and we laughed with joy and relief. Lizzie even though she had started to come round she was still very poorly, on drips, heart monitors, and everything you could think of and was quite scary.

Her potassium levels weren't right because of the swine flu and all the complications they also found out that her kidneys were failing so she was on a dialysis machine, but at least we had Lizzie back she over the next couple of days and she was coming round and talking a bit more although still not her usual bubbly self because was very poorly still. Next came the decision to move her out of intensive care to Doncaster royal Infirmary where she was on dialysis but at least she could have her friends to and see her a real bonus of the ever-sociable Lizzie! She spent three weeks in Doncaster hospital and while the staff were fantastic, they were still not sure what was going to happen with her as the kidneys were still not working.

Lizzie was such a petit young woman at only five feet nothing Lizzie began to suffer from swelling and her normal size 8 became an unfamiliar size 14 and she was not at all happy about that side effect of the problem with her kidneys! Her birthday was fast approaching on the 6th of December, and we had spoken to the doctors about seeing if we could bring her home even just for the weekend. Although initially doubtful on the 4th of December they agreed we could bring her home, but with trips back for dialysis and we were given strict instructions on her care. I shot into town to get her some leggings and sweatshirts because nothing would fit, so that she could come home and in spite everything it was wonderful.

Still poorly she could not do very much, but it was just so good to have her home. Her birthday may have been a quieter celebration than she was used to. Grandparents, family, friends visited, and it seemed to be the start of an improvement enough for her to stay out of hospital and be able to move around more she seemed start losing some of the fluid, during the day we had to go back to work. Lizzie was collected by her grandma during the day so that she was not alone. She was walking around a bit more and everything seemed to start coming into place and so the fluid started draining off and when mummy and Barry took her to the hospital for her check-ups, they did some tests for her kidneys, and they said that everything was starting to work again.

So come the middle of December after a quiet family Christmas and New Year spent enjoying time with Lizzie, I finally heard my lovely, brave daughter had been given all clear, wonderful news! Life could begin again! Back to work and of course Lizzie being a party animal began with a much-needed celebration with her friends, people who had supported her with visits in hospital and others she hadn't seen for weeks. It was one of her special friend's birthday Sebina who she had known since they were toddlers. The next day I had to wake her up to give me a hand in the house and to hear all about her night out, she was so happy as she had seen lots of people and I could see my Lizzie back to herself. I popped to Lorraine's, my best friend who was the mum of Sebina to drop off a present for all the family. There was a lovely of things getting back to normal as I chatted with my close friend. My husband Garry and I even made plans to go out for the afternoon and do something that we used to do before all this happened. While we were out, I had a text from Lizzie, telling me she was going to go out with her other girlfriend Emily. Still not quite easy about Lizzie I asked when and where she was going and she replied, "oh I am not sure I am like you can't make my mind up, but I'll let you know later".

Lizzie was 20 by now and while I knew I was being over protected the recent events had made me more careful of things somehow. But was reassured because she always communicated well with me.

That text was the last time I ever heard from Lizzie. I had come home from the drink with Garry, as I remember alone as he stayed in the pub drinking which wasn't unusual. I went to bed somehow, I could not sleep I kept checking my phone it seemed strange that she hadn't contacted me, I tried to get hold of her, but I couldn't, I told myself that her phone had run out of battery and that she had gone to her friends. Maybe she decided to stay overnight, and she would contact me in the morning.

I must have drifted off and about 5:00 o'clock in the morning my mobile rang, not a number I knew so, I asked who it was, and they said it was the police. It is the worst phone call I have had and will ever have in my life. They asked me if Lizzie was at home at home, I stumbled to double check her room in case I had not heard her creep in. I said no I've been waiting for her to come home I had drifted off. They explained there had been they think a car accident and I said, "Well have you checked the hospitals". and they said they'll come round and see us. I knew things were bad I woke my husband up and told him the police were on the way with something to do with Lizzie it's not good.

Within 15-20 minutes there was a knock at the door two policemen came in said that had been a car accident and could they have a photograph of Lizzie because they wanted to use it to see if she had been seen anywhere? In a haze I handed them a recent photograph form the top of the cabinet in the lounge. They took the photograph away and came back far too quickly. They said they were deeply sorry, but Lizzie had been involved in a car accident and unfortunately both girls Lizzie and her friend Emily had died. I didn't know what to do or how to act, I went into autopilot saying we have to contact people we had to tell people that our beloved lizzie had died. My husband began the dreadful process of contacting family members because I just couldn't. I knew they were words I couldn't speak to people who loved her so much. I couldn't cause them that much pain. Garry phoned my brother James because I couldn't tell my parents he then phoned his brother who I believe told his parents. I kept calling my best friend Lorraine and eventually got hold of her. As always, she came straight around, always a support and always a star- normally for girls' nights out but this time to accompany us to identify Lizzies body at the morgue. it was harrowing we learned that the girls had drowned as the car had gone over a small bridge where there was usually a stream, but recent bad weather had flooded it. Lizzies dear little body was back to like it was when she was in hospital full of fluid.

I wandered round a lost soul for quite a while not knowing what to do. The police were excellent, and we had a support person that kept in touch and went through everything. The other young girl involved Lizzie's friend Emily was driving. I knew Emily from staying at our house so many times after nights out or raucous sleepovers, but we had never met her parents.

The police had said that Emily's parents wished to meet us I remember meeting and I know we did but I can't remember a thing about it weirdly, like something out of an odd dream or film-whatever can we have talked about? I remember they took us for a Chinese a few days afterwards which was truly kind of them. We met up again when family and friends went to the crash site to pay our respects and set off Chinese lanterns.

Looking back, it was the wrong thing to do for me, why did I go? Probably to keep the peace, you do many things on autopilot when you lose somebody like this, I didn't know how to react to anything or how to get through each day. I do remember smoking and drinking far too much and my husband going for lots of walks and being very distant.

We then had the local press coming round they wanted a story, they popped notes through neighbours' doors wanting information about Lizzie. I remember the local reporter coming to the door the next day or maybe the day after I cannot exactly remember what day it was, but they asked for information I shouted and swore at them telling to leave my house, they should not do this sort of thing it is very upsetting. Somewhere in my head I decided to take control. They wanted a story well I would tell them about Lizzie. I did not want anybody else to talk about her she was our daughter and I needed to speak about her myself. We walked down to the Retford Times and asked to see a reporter about the accident, they were incredibly surprised but pleased that we had come to the office. We talked about Lizzie explaining what a wonderful young lady she was and how vivacious she was and how well she had been doing in both work and college because that is what she was, an amazing young lady and that is the way I want everyone to remember her.

Next came the funeral, I have never had anybody close to me die so did not really know what to do we were taken through the process by an old Retford company Hurtons, Retford is such a small town, and they knew the story before we got there. They gently guided us through the process, amazingly maybe because Lizzie had been so poorly, we'd talked about death, and she told me she wanted to be cremated it was good to know for sure. What parent knows how their child wants their body to be dealt with after death! She was quite different because as Lizzie said, "I don't want the worms eating me".

I knew I didn't want a big hard coffin she was a petit young woman, so we chose something beautiful made from wicker with a very a basic Lilly spray on top.

One of Lizzies favourite teachers was the Reverend Ferriter so we asked her if she could do the service at the crematorium. We contacted Felicity to explain what had happened and if she would do the service. The strangest thing was she had a reading to do on the day it was Lizzie's own work about death and making the most of life utterly amazing. She loved Religious Studies and Lizzie had written a piece of work about life and dying, Felicity had kept the work to show other students who were getting ready for their exams. Listening to this at Lizzies funeral really was surreal. Felicity read that out on the actual day of the funeral the strange world we live in.

Between the organising and the funeral was ten days. A void of time and attempts to numb a pain of such intensity it made it hard. I drank, smoked cried much of the time I was alone. My husband kept disappearing, obviously very heartbroken, and we did not seem able to handle it together very well at all. The day of the funeral arrived, and everybody came over a hundred people there it was amazing, just a wonderful send-off no more than my beautiful girl deserved.

The following day we had Emily's funeral as well, so it was incredibly sad time for all their friends and family, the clergy of Retford were amazing and supported the young friends throughout the day. I really struggled on the day; Emily's funeral was completely different form Lizzies. It was at a church in Retford and Emily arrived in a horse drawn carriage. Emily was buried after the service. I couldn’t attend this as it was all too much for me.

In the days that followed we had to look at our life, what to do next, how to go on Lizzie was our only child. I found I couldn't go into her room I just couldn't do it and after just another week I had to go back to work I hated going back because that was where I was when Lizzie was taken ill. Driving to and from work each day I cried my eyes out. I managed to be strong when in the office and put a work head on, the team were incredibly supportive I couldn’t have asked for anymore.

After a few weeks I decided to start looking for another job because I just couldn't settle as I was driving there it used to give me bad vibes all the time making me even sadder.

At home things were even worse than at work, I couldn’t really expect work colleagues to understand but surely my husband Lizzies daddy and I could grieve together. Life was not normal we went out met up with friends had meals.

The one thing I did notice was on a regular basis my husband was working later and getting lots of call outs, so I spent a lot of time alone. I just thought is this what the rest of my life is going to be like. I really hoped it wasn't, I did not want the death of Lizzie to be the death of myself as this made me feel like her life would have been wasted and that would have been so sad.

I used to visit Lizzies grave regularly as we had her ashes put into Retford Cemetery so that we and her friends and other family members had somewhere to go and chat to her. Sitting here I felt closer I needed somewhere to go, even though I couldn't go into her bedroom I felt calm when at her grave even though I cried at most visits.

In March we went away as my parents had bought a weekend break as a Christmas gift. It was such a sad weekend because we knew we were going to have to go home to an empty house. Again, my husband was on the phone a lot during the few days for work, so we did not get any proper time and we did not talk about things properly. We came home and I was determined to get a new job which I did. I updated my CV and put it on all the recruitment sites. It didn't take long to get an interview and I started my new job in the April, it was great because it kept me busy. I was running the membership of four health clubs it really kept me occupied, I was coping as I always put on a strong front, I spoke about Lizzie and did not break down very often and I started to feel stronger, looking back now I knew I was masking a lot of sadness. My husband though had continued drinking an awful lot and I know I had a few probably more than I would have done usually. It had started to cause arguments, he would not talk to me, all he kept saying is that it was because of the death of Lizzie why he was acting as he was. I remember talking to friends saying how worried I was about Garry as he was bottling everything up and acting very oddly, I was truly worried as he often said he didn't want to be alive anymore. He wouldn't speak to anyone.

It was a May bank holiday we had been invited out as friends were over from Iceland, it started off as a nice time then Garry started drinking and being nasty with the way he was talking to me, he was very snappy and condescending so I said I cannot cope with this anymore I am going home. I wasn't staying around somebody who couldn't be pleasant he needed to remember I was hurting too. Others noticed the way he was and asked if he was ok, I explained that he was grieving as that was what he always told me. It was because of the death of Lizzie he always said. He came back late that night plastered. He got up Sunday morning and disappeared I thought he had gone to get the paper or shopping; he did not answer any calls or texts. I was extremely worried; I contacted his friends to see if they had seen him. I really wasn't sure what to do. He eventually came back after quite a few hours, I said to him "where have you been what is happening". He said "I don't love anything or you anymore" I asked to talk, and he just walked out of the house again. I was in shock; we had been together for about twenty-eight years. I thought I knew him. How wrong was I. Eventually I sent him a text as he wasn't answering his phone, I said are you having an affair. I still don't know why I asked this, it must had been my 6th sense he sent me one back and said YES, wow well I had lost Lizzie that was the worst thing that I could ever have happened. So, I calmly went upstairs packed my bag walked out the house and into my car and drove down to my parents and said can I stay for a few days I have left Garry. My parents were amazing, they asked a few questions obviously but all they wanted to know was that I was ok.

It was three months before our 25th wedding anniversary but I was not staying somewhere and being treated like this. the worst thing that ever happened to me was losing my daughter & I have got the rest of my life I need to live it as happily as I can. I was worried about him because he had been so low, I was getting his friends to talk to him because I was worried, he was going to do something to himself. There all this time he was going out and seeing this other woman and having an affair. It had been going on for quite a few months I found out later. So, while

Lizzie was in an induced coma in hospital with swine flu, he was going to see this woman. It still to this day amazes me that a woman who also had children acted this way when she knew that he had a daughter in hospital on a life support machine at the beginning of the affair and then she knew Lizzie had been killed in a car accident, but she carried on the affair amazing! It also explained why on the day of the funeral he disappeared. He had said to me he needed to clear his head, so I had to deal with all the mourners that came to our house alone.

Right, this was Monday morning my start of my new life. I went into work, and I spoke to my line manager and explained I had left my husband and said I might need a few days off now and again because I need to sort everything out. I had left my two dogs at the house, and he was not the kindest of persons with the dogs so I said to my mummy can I bring them back here just for a couple of days until I find myself somewhere to live. She said of course so I texted him and said I need to come and get some paperwork as I need to rent a house. I also need to pick the dogs up.

I found out that he had taken the oldest dog to be put down without even going through it with me, like I said he was not the nicest people. I really should have left years previously, but I really didn't want Lizzie to be form a broken family as she did love her daddy. I picked up my Beagle and the paperwork I needed and left that house.

It was a frantic week. I had to find a solicitor because I wanted a divorce immediately and then to find a house, as luck would have it, I found this one bedroom back-to-back little house that sounded ideal, and I had lived close and in the same style house when I first moved to Retford with my husband. I contacted the people that were renting the house out and explained that I have got a dog explained my situation and they were amazing and agreed I could move in, so I got it all arranged for that Saturday.

I texted my husband and said that I need to go and get some clothes from the house, and I did not want him to be there. I said I would text him once, I had finished in the house and that was it. I wrote a list out of what I was going to take out of the house. I went through room by room. Again, Lorraine and her husband Tig came up trumps and along with my parents and brother we set about getting my things for my new life. I had made a list of what I was taking from each room. Each person went into a room getting things from the list. Lizzie's room I still could not go in, so my best friend Lorraine and mummy went in there for me. Since the death of Lizzie, I had only been in her room twice before, one to get an outfit to take to the undertakers and the second was to see if the room would help me but, on both occasions, I got so upset as memories of the last time I saw her in there came flooding back. My plan was to leave it as it was for as long as possible, but due to her daddy's infidelity I wasn't going to be able to. I took all her furniture because my father had made that for her and there is no way on earth that was staying in that house. I also took all the pictures off the wall because I did not feel he was worthy of having pictures of Lizzie the way he had acted over the last six months was unbelievable he hadn't thought of his daughter obviously because if he had he would be by her bedside and indulging in an adulterous affair. I did leave the family photos though, so that he had his memories of what he had lost.

It did not take long to get what I needed, I was incredibly good you could not tell I had been in in the house apart from a couple of ornaments that I wanted and the gaps on the walls. I left the house Immaculate. We then went and set up my new little home which was my haven and straight away I loved it. It was my tranquil haven and I felt at ease there. I had pictures of Lizzie around me I could come and go as I pleased, and I can say I did feel very calm there I settled into my new life. Mummy found me a solicitor and I set the ball rolling for a divorce Garry did not want to admit to anything for quite a while and used to tell people I had left him, missing out the reason why, all I can presume was that he was a tad embarrassed about the way he had acted, I do honestly hope so. I could not find the woman's name at the time and after many letters going to and fro he would eventually sign the papers admitting that he had been having an affair and so we got the divorce on adultery. It took a long time because he was not very forthcoming in sending information that we needed. I was going out in the evenings again with Lorraine and Tig and starting to enjoy my life obviously I had exceptionally low moments and I would go and sit up at the cemetery and talk to Liz, I told her what had happened and that her daddy had found another family, however I had got a lovely new house and that I was sure she would have loved it.

In the spring I met somebody that I knew to say hello to because I used to live next door but one to him. He asked me if I would like to go out on a date. This was in June, so I had not even left a month. "Oh, crikey am I ready" I thought that you only have one life and there is nothing to lose so he picked me up one evening we went to the pub, and we talked and talked and talked. It was amazing we had so much in common, the same music doing and enjoying the same pastimes. He obviously knew about Lizzie, and he remembered her from when we use to live next door, but she was only little when we left. I used to see him around town, and we would say hello and that was it nothing else I did not know any of what his life really entailed, or anything. We started to see each other regularly going out doing lots of walking, just being together. Then Steve asked me if I would like to go on holiday with him, I had not been abroad for years. I did not even have a passport, so I thought what I have got to lose, I sent off for my passport and then at the end of August we went on holiday. Steve wanted to go for two weeks, and I had never done a two-week holiday not for years and years, so I said let us just go for a week to see how things go. To see how we get on together. The whole week was fantastic the best I have ever had, it was amazing, and we have never looked back. I started staying more and more at Steve's. We met each other's parents & friends and continued to have great fun outings doing things we both love. I felt like I had found my true soul mate. My biggest sadness was that Lizzie never got to know Steve, I know she would have loved him and he her too. Christmas came round which was the first Christmas without Lizzie. I wanted to do something completely different, and Steve's sister had invited us there which was truly kind of her, and it took my mind off the sadness of the day. it was it was awfully hard from the start of Christmas as I always spoilt Lizzie with lots of gifts and outings to the shops beforehand. Then on the morning we used to all go down together to open presents. However, Steve and his family made it lovely for me. Steve accepted me talking about Lizzie and he comes with me to the cemetery to see her and so my life sort of got back on track.

We started to discuss me moving in as I spent more and more time at Steve's as my little house as lovely as it was it was extremely cold as the winter was unbelievably bad, we had lots of snow. I moved in with Steve in the middle of January seven months form when we first started dating. This probably seems fast to some, but I can honestly say I have never felt so happy and contented as when I am with Steve, and you only have one life.

We started our new life; I still cannot believe it to this day, and I mean we are now talking eleven years ago how one man could change me from being a very unhappy person into somebody that realised the relationship she had had for nearly 25 years was bad.

But until you get out of situations you do not know what situation you are in. In the February time I was incredibly low everything started to hit me, and I think because I was relaxing more because I was so happy everything got on top of me, and I needed some time out which I had needed for a long time. Steve just said right give up work take a few months off and get your head straight, so I did. I had about three months off which was especially good I did some decorating, baking, things I enjoyed. Steve loved it because obviously I was looking after him and I loved it because he was looking after me.

When I was looking for another job, I decided not to go back into management doing lots of hours I needed to have more time at home and something less stressful. I went to work for a company called AVN doing their administration side of things which was fantastic just what I needed, it was easy to do, and I did it for just under a year. I needed this time as I then felt able to start doing other things.

I always have talked about Lizzie, and she was always the forefront of everything eventually after I think it was 18 months, I managed to get my divorce through. Even though the breakdown of the marriage had been promoted by the affair it cost a great deal for me to end it which very unfair really seeing it was Garry that had the affair. There is one thing even though after being hurt and used as I was within that relationship I have never once not trusted Steve. All the years that I was married to Garry, I did not trust him so much, but I think because of Lizzie I was afraid I didn't want to upset the family unit which when I look back at, I wish I had, because he didn't deserve to have a wonderful daughter who thought the world of him especially the way he treated Lizzie in the last few months of her life. Now I have had a chance to look back I do think that

Garry was a sad person, due to his up bringing and family struggles that he had impacted on our lives.

In the next few years, I changed my job several times finding the new me and what I wanted to do. The one thing I did not do was speak to a councillor or coach about what had happened to me. Within six months I had lost my daughter my home my then husband, changed jobs found a new relationship. The relationship was the best thing that happened to me as Steve gave me the love and support that I truly needed to rebuild my life.

This is a lot for the body and mind to take in and I kept getting poorly and was always at the doctors. My mummy & aunty Jo kept saying to me look you need to go and speak to somebody and all I would say is "no I am alright". I always wanted to put the brave face on.

My auntie who is a health kinesiologist, this is when they use gentle muscle testing combined with verbal questioning to communicate directly with your body's unique energy system suggested to my mummy that I go and speak to another kinesiologist as she said that it would help. When it was first mentioned to me, I said no I am fine, Jo had said that when she is ready, she will go and see someone. Then one day I think it was in the summer 2013. I thought no it is time to do something about this, so I contacted the therapist and basically for three hours I spoke about my childhood my relationship with them my now ex-husband the loss of Lizzie sadness, everything that was making me unhappy. I came out looking like I had done ten rounds with a Tyson Fury. My eyes were bloodshot, but I felt so much lighter.

I could see a way forward and I realised how great talking is when you are feeling grief especially the multiple grief, I was coping with I was grieving over the loss of Lizzie the loss of our marriage lost my house the loss of my dogs. because I had lost my dogs by then as well.

So, after that day going forward, I decided I wanted to help myself and others, I started doing courses I did a Life Coaching Diploma course. I did Coaching and Mentoring courses, I also did a Counselling course, I read every book on grief I could get my hands on and how it affects people and eventually my plan was to help others that are struggling through life's turmoil's.

Then in 2014 Steve proposed to me and we set the wedding for the 21st of May 2016.

I had lots of planning to do, Steven had never been married before, so he wanted to have quite a big wedding and I wanted to have a better one than the one before! We decided to get married at the in a beautiful hotel with gardens meaning we could realise my dream of having the ceremony outside. The day eventually came, and even though it was raining, and Steve gave the decision that it was going to be outside, because he knew how much it meant to me.

I walked down to Steve on the arm of my stepfather Barry a wonderful man to Open Arms by Journey. Steve was waiting.

We managed to have Lizzie with us "in spirit by making sure we partied (almost) as hard as she would have done, we had her friends with us, and we drank a toast of apple sour shots- which were truly disgusting and exactly what we all needed to help us laugh.

The wonderful Felicity who did Lizzie's funeral bought everything together for us by blessing our rings.

We left the next day for Mexico for a two-week honeymoon. I had never done long haul before and never been to anywhere like that it was just all magical we came home and started living married life.

We always have fun, and we go away lots. I moved Jobs again!! I found one loved I became a coach to apprentices, training them in customer service ready for their exams, helping others it was my passion. But the company went bust! Not to be defeated I found another one with a similar role and learned some new skills.

Married life was brilliant we did lots we bought a motorbike and have fun in the sun popping out for the evenings or nipping to the seaside at the weekend, then biking had to end as we decided to get a puppy, well I had really wanted one for years and I managed to badger

Steve into it, After the bike went, we bought a lovely red sports car to carry the three of us in. In 2019 after a holiday on a narrowboat with Steve's family a new dream was borne when we agreed we'd like to live on a narrowboat when we retire. that was it.

We went to have a look at some boats, and we could not really find one that we liked or that we did not have to do lots of work on to make it to a home. Steve then said let's get our own boat built to our design, we can afford it and it will be our home. Steve planned it out carefully by reading articles and information form his many narrowboat books and using his memories of previous holidays he had had with his family. I also had my input with the design also. We found these fantastic people at XR&D to build it.

The build began in July 2020 I realised I needed to simplify my work life to be able to enjoy the project so the opportunity to reach my dream came up and MKB Life Coach evolved from I thought I want something else as well to go alongside that as I am building my coaching business so The Floating VA was born because then I can run both businesses whilst living on the narrowboat.

January the 4th 2021 I handed my notice in, it was a scary thing to do but with support from Steve and self-belief I made the changes. I now run both the businesses and have reduced how many hours a week I work so that I can spend time with loved ones. My main aim is to run the Life Coaching business, specialising in grief and bereavement. The reason for this is I have been there, and I have a better understanding, also helping with relationships because again I have been there. I have an amazing understanding of what its like to go through traumas in your life. I have written this story so you understand that **YES** tough times do happen, but you can come out the other side. I do not want people reading this book to feel sad for what has happened, I want you to embrace your lives with the support of the journal and start to live your life after whatever type of trauma you have been through because you only have one life, please do not waste it.

Now following the next **31 days** and building your self-confidence back up and asking for help you too will be able to see the light at the end of the tunnel. You too will be able to build an amazing life. It does take some time and it can be incredibly stressful but never ever give up. My mantra is to remember it is always OK to be OK. Do not let people think that you should be sad all the time. You should not let the person that you have lost or the things that you are grieving for ruin your life. Grief can be from the loss of a loved one, a relationship break-up be it a partner or a friendship, the death of a beloved pet or even the loss of your job. This is your life now. You have amazing memories, and they will never ever leave you, but it is time now to make new memories and go forward.

Thank you.

Maxine x

How to use the 31-day Journal

This journal is for you to use exactly how you want the following information are ideas, but only you will know exactly what you need and what works for you.

I write my journal each morning after I have been for my walk. I write what happened the previous day and how I am feeling also how I am feeling at the present time.

I say my affirmations and choose my positive word of statement for the day ahead.

Meditation also plays a big part of my life these days and I do this at all different times depending on how I am feeling. I have found meditation to be a great way of getting back on track especially if I am feeling agitated or sad.

One thing I must say is if you happen to miss a day, please do not beat yourself up, just the next day start again and get back on track. Its not a failure its just a slight deviation from your new life.

Day 1:

Affirmation:

I believe that this new change in my life shall bring endless opportunities for me.

Journal:

Today's Positive Word:

Day 2:

Affirmation:

My life will change with this new beginning, in a positive way.

Journal:

Today's Positive Word:

Day 3:

Affirmation:

I am going to live the best chapter of my life, from now.

Journal:

Today's Positive Word:

Day 4:

Affirmation:

This new phase of my life will help me grow as a human being.

Journal:

Today's Positive Word:

Day 5:

Affirmation:

I am now ready for a new start.

Journal:

Today's Positive Word:

Day 6:

Affirmation:

I deserve to have a happy fulfilled life.

Journal:

Today's Positive Word:

Day 7:

Affirmation:

I am about to rediscover myself with this fresh start.

Journal:

Today's Positive Word:

Day 8:

Affirmation:

I shall be the chauffeur of my life in this new beginning.

Journal:

Today's Positive Word:

Day 9:

Affirmation:

If I’m anxious that’s ok, I’ll move forward anyway?

Journal:

Today’s Positive Word:

Day 10:

Affirmation:

I will get worried, but I will not let this apprehension guide me in this new chapter of my life.

Journal:

Today's Positive Word:

Day 11:

Affirmation:

I am brave to have taken this choice.

Journal:

Today's Positive Word:

Day 12:

Affirmation:

I accept my new beginning with open arms and heart.

Journal:

Today's Positive Word:

Day 13:

Affirmation:

I race to meet the good things coming my way.

Journal:

Today's Positive Word:

Day 14:

Affirmation:

I shall work harder than ever to get to the place where I want to be.

Journal:

Today's Positive Word:

Day 15:

Affirmation:

This new phase brings with it heaps of belief and contentment in my life.

Journal:

Today's Positive Word:

Day 16:

Affirmation:

I am distancing myself from all kinds of negativity and just going to focus on my growth.

Journal:

Today's Positive Word:

Day 17:

Affirmation:

This fresh start was indeed very vital for me to move forward.

Journal:

Today's Positive Word:

Day 18:

Affirmation:

I jump out of my comfort zone into this new part of life.

Journal:

Today's Positive Word:

Day 19:

Affirmation:

This new happiness place is where I belong.

Journal:

Today's Positive Word:

Day 20:

Affirmation:

I shall go for quality in this new stage of my life and let success follow me.

Journal:

Today's Positive Word:

Day 21:

Affirmation:

I am finding myself and starting a fresh.

Journal:

Today's Positive Word:

Day 22:

Affirmation:

I am joyful about this fresh start.

Journal:

Today's Positive Word:

Day 23:

Affirmation:

My life changes, while I cherish my wonderful memories.

Journal:

Today's Positive Word:

Day 24:

Affirmation:

I am a confident person.

Journal:

Today's Positive Word:

Day 25:

Affirmation:

I continue to grow and develop in my new life.

Journal:

Today's Positive Word:

Day 26:

Affirmation:

I am kind to myself each day.

Journal:

Today's Positive Word:

Day 27:

Affirmation:

I am worthy of a happy life.

Journal:

Today's Positive Word:

Day 28:

Affirmation:

I will a smile on my face at the start of each day.

Journal:

Today's Positive Word:

Day 29:

Affirmation:

I give myself permission to be happy and let go of the past.

Journal:

Today's Positive Word:

Day 30:

Affirmation:

I live each day how I want to.

Journal:

Today's Positive Word:

Day 31:

Affirmation:

I treat each day as a new beginning in my life.

Journal:

Today's Positive Word:

A few Lessons

Lesson- Dream big it will come to you

Lesson: Life isn't fair- you must be prepared to suck somethings up to get the outcome

Lesson – Take action to grow your dream,

Lesson- Keep changing until it feels right. Each step gets you nearer

Lesson- Keeping your loved one present at key moments, laugh/ celebrate is so important

Notes for you.

Useful links.

Book a free chemistry call with myself

https://calendly.com/mkblifecoach/30min

www.mkblifecoach.com

Webinar to help you.

https://webinarkit.com/webinar/605b4d672d35c1001712a558

Recommended Reading List

Mindfulness for Your Success by Katie Black

Johnathan Livingston Seagull by Richard Bach

Meditation Channels

https://youtu.be/Xx6gj6RLRdg Relaxation

https://youtu.be/jeGT1VXwfx4 Positive Energy

https://youtu.be/ZToicYcHIOU Calming.

https://youtu.be/UONvpzG7yjo Relaxing Sleep music

Facebook

https://www.facebook.com/MKBlifecoach

Twitter

@LifeMkb

Printed in Great Britain
by Amazon

64557367R00047